AF510105

Tax Relief's Realization

Practical strategies for addressing financial burdens through tax forgiveness programs, hardship waivers and alternative payment arrangements

Maxwell Langdon

Contents

1 Introduction to Tax Relief **5**
1.1 Understanding Tax Burdens 7
1.2 Exploring Relief Options 8

2 Tax Forgiveness Programs **11**
2.1 Eligibility Criteria 13
2.2 Application Process 14
2.3 Success Stories 16

3 Hardship Waivers & Appeals **19**
3.1 Demonstrating Hardship 21
3.2 Preparing Appeals 22

4 Installment Agreements **25**
4.1 Setting Up Payments 27
4.2 Managing Installments 28
4.3 Potential Penalties 30
4.4 Modifying Agreements 32
4.5 Defaulting on Agreements 34

5 Offer in Compromise (OIC) **37**
5.1 OIC Eligibility 39
5.2 Negotiating an OIC 41
5.3 Acceptance & Rejection 42

6 Alternative Payment Options . . . 45
6.1 Short-Term Options . . . 47
6.2 Long-Term Strategies . . . 49
6.3 Seeking Professional Help . . . 51

7 Conclusion: Securing Your Financial Future . . . 53
7.1 Maintaining Tax Compliance . . . 55
7.2 Planning for the Future . . . 57

1 Introduction to Tax Relief

Facing a significant tax burden can be overwhelming, but understanding the available options is the first step towards resolution. Many individuals and businesses find themselves struggling under the weight of unpaid taxes, leading to stress, anxiety, and even legal repercussions. However, numerous avenues exist for obtaining tax relief, offering a path toward financial stability. Knowing where to begin and what resources to utilize is crucial.
Relief isn't a one-size-fits-all solution; the appropriate approach depends significantly on your specific circumstances and the nature of your tax debt. Factors such as the amount owed, the length of time the debt has been outstanding, your income, and assets all play a role in determining eligibility for various programs. For example, someone with a relatively small tax debt might qualify for an installment agreement, while someone with a substantial debt and demonstrable financial hardship might pursue an Offer in Compromise (OIC).
Navigating the complexities of tax relief often requires careful consideration and, frequently, professional assistance. Tax laws are intricate and constantly evolving, making independent interpretation challenging and potentially risky. Enlisting the services of a tax professional, such as an enrolled agent or tax attorney, can significantly improve your chances of success. They possess in-depth knowledge of tax codes, regulations, and procedures, allowing them to guide you through the process effectively. Their expertise can save you time, money, and unnecessary stress, ensuring you're employing the most appropriate strategies for your situation.
Tax forgiveness programs, for instance, offer a potential path to eliminating tax debt entirely. These programs often target individuals facing exceptional financial hardship or those who have made honest mistakes in their tax filings.

Eligibility criteria can vary, however, requiring careful review and documentation to substantiate your claim. The application process itself can be demanding, often involving extensive paperwork and meticulous record-keeping. Success depends on accurately presenting your case and demonstrating your need for relief.

Understanding the nuances of hardship waivers and appeals is equally important. Proving financial hardship is more than simply stating you're struggling; you need substantial evidence to support your claim. This might include bank statements, pay stubs, medical bills, and other documentation demonstrating your inability to pay your tax liabilities. Preparing a compelling appeal necessitates a clear and concise presentation of your case, highlighting the reasons for your financial difficulties and demonstrating your willingness to resolve the situation. An effective appeal requires a strategic approach, meticulously presenting facts and evidence to support your request.

An installment agreement allows you to repay your tax debt in manageable installments, providing a structured repayment plan that alleviates immediate financial pressure. However, carefully understanding the terms and conditions is vital. Late payments can trigger penalties and interest, potentially negating the benefits of the agreement. Maintaining consistent payments is crucial for successfully completing the installment agreement. Failure to do so could result in further complications and additional penalties.

Beyond installment agreements and tax forgiveness programs, alternative payment options offer flexibility in managing tax debt. These options often include short-term strategies like short-term payment plans or long-term options focusing on financial rehabilitation and responsible debt management. Consider exploring these options only after careful evaluation and, ideally, with professional guidance. Remember, a sustainable solution is one that addresses both the immediate and long-term financial implications.

Ultimately, securing your financial future requires not only addressing current tax liabilities but also establishing proactive strategies for tax compliance and responsible financial management. Regularly reviewing your finances, maintaining accurate records, and seeking professional guidance are invaluable steps in avoiding future tax problems. By incorporating these practices into your financial routine, you'll significantly reduce the likelihood of facing similar challenges in the future. Remember, proactive planning is the best defense against overwhelming tax burdens.

1.1 Understanding Tax Burdens

Understanding your tax burden is the first step towards navigating the complexities of tax relief. It's not just about the sheer number on your tax bill; it's about understanding the underlying components and how they impact your overall financial health. This involves recognizing not just federal income tax, but also state and local taxes, property taxes, sales taxes, and any other levies imposed on your income, assets, or transactions. Failing to comprehend the full scope of your tax obligations can lead to unforeseen financial difficulties. A comprehensive understanding is crucial for identifying potential avenues for relief.

The calculation of your tax burden involves several key elements. Your adjusted gross income (AGI) is a critical factor, representing your gross income less certain deductions. Tax deductions, such as those for charitable contributions or mortgage interest, directly reduce your taxable income, thus lowering your overall tax burden. Tax credits, unlike deductions, directly reduce your tax liability, providing more significant relief. For example, the Earned Income Tax Credit (EITC) offers substantial tax relief to low-to-moderate-income working individuals and families. Understanding the interplay between these factors is paramount to accurately assessing your tax situation.

Moreover, the tax rates applicable to your income bracket play a significant role in determining your tax burden. Progressive tax systems, like the one in the United States, impose higher tax rates on higher income levels. Therefore, a thorough understanding of your income bracket and the corresponding tax rates is crucial. This also extends to capital gains taxes, which are levied on profits from investments. Different asset classes are subject to varying tax rates, impacting your overall tax liability. Careful consideration of these rates is essential when making financial decisions.

Beyond income tax, numerous other taxes can significantly contribute to your overall tax burden. Property taxes, levied on real estate, can be substantial, especially for homeowners. Sales taxes, imposed on goods and services, add to the cost of everyday purchases, gradually increasing your overall tax outlay. Estate and gift taxes, levied on large inheritances and gifts, can have significant implications for high-net-worth individuals and families. Neglecting these taxes in your overall assessment can lead to inaccurate financial planning.

Furthermore, the intricacies of tax laws often result in unexpected tax liabilities. These can stem from changes in tax legislation, specific circumstances, or interpretations of the tax code. For instance, the complexities of international tax regulations can lead to unexpected tax bills for individuals with international income or assets. Therefore, maintaining detailed records, understanding applicable legislation, and seeking professional guidance when needed are vital to avoid such surprises. Proactive planning and informed decision-making are key to mitigating such risks. This requires staying updated on tax laws and regulations, which can be a significant challenge given their complexity and frequent amendments.

Ignoring or misinterpreting these aspects can lead to substantial financial problems. Overlooking certain deductions or credits could result in overpaying taxes, leading to unnecessary financial strain. Failing to account for all applicable taxes can lead to penalties and interest charges, further compounding the financial burden. An accurate assessment of your tax burden forms the foundation for effective tax planning and the exploration of various relief options. It's crucial to assemble all necessary financial documentation: tax returns, pay stubs, investment statements, and any other relevant documents. This thorough preparation streamlines the process of calculating your overall tax burden and allows for a more accurate assessment. A clear picture of your tax liability is fundamental in your quest for tax relief. Remember, proactive planning and a thorough understanding are invaluable assets in managing your financial well-being.

1.2 Exploring Relief Options

Delving into tax relief can feel overwhelming, a maze of jargon and complicated procedures. But understanding the options available is the first step towards resolving your tax burden. Remember, you're not alone; many individuals face similar challenges. The crucial thing is to take proactive steps, seeking information and professional help when needed. Don't let the complexity paralyze you.

Finding the right relief option depends significantly on your specific circumstances. Your income level, the nature of your tax debt, and the assets you possess all play a crucial role in determining your eligibility for different programs. For instance, if you're facing a temporary hardship, a short-term payment plan might suffice. However, if you're dealing with a substantial tax debt and limited resources, an Offer in Compromise (OIC) might be a more appropriate strategy. Careful consideration of your individual financial standing is paramount.

Consider the IRS's Fresh Start initiative. Designed to assist taxpayers struggling with tax debt, it encompasses several relief programs, including installment agreements and OICs. Understanding the nuances of these programs is vital. Each program has specific eligibility requirements and procedures. Familiarizing yourself with these details empowers you to make informed decisions. Failing to understand the criteria can lead to rejection of your application. This can cause further delays and potential penalties.

Navigating the process alone can be daunting. Many find the IRS's procedures complex and challenging to interpret. Seeking advice from a qualified tax professional can significantly improve your chances of success. They can not only help you determine the most suitable relief option but also guide you through the application process, ensuring compliance with all regulations and maximizing your chances of a favorable outcome. Their expertise is invaluable in streamlining the process and achieving a resolution. This professional support is an investment worth making for many, ensuring they receive proper guidance.

Remember, accurate record-keeping is crucial throughout this process. Maintaining meticulous records of income, expenses, and tax documentation not only streamlines the application procedure for any relief program you pursue but also provides crucial evidence in support of your claim. These documents are essential in demonstrating your financial situation accurately to tax authorities. This level of precision can be the difference between approval and rejection.

The emotional toll of dealing with tax debt shouldn't be underestimated. The stress and anxiety associated with financial burdens can negatively affect your mental and physical well-being. Remember to prioritize self-care throughout this process. Seek support from friends, family, or mental health professionals if needed. This ensures you stay focused and proactive. Taking care of yourself is paramount for navigating the challenges ahead effectively. Your mental state plays a crucial role in the success of your endeavor.

Don't feel pressured to make hasty decisions. Take your time to explore your options and choose the one best suited to your situation. Rushing into a decision can lead to unforeseen consequences, particularly when dealing with complicated tax laws and regulations. A well-informed decision made after careful deliberation greatly increases the probability of a favorable outcome. This methodical approach demonstrates responsibility and respect for the process involved.

Finally, remember that securing tax relief isn't just about resolving current debts. It's also about establishing a solid foundation for your future financial well-being. Once your tax issues are resolved, focus on implementing proactive strategies for managing your finances. This includes creating a realistic budget, tracking expenses, and seeking professional financial guidance if necessary. This approach ensures that you prevent future financial difficulties and maintain long-term tax compliance. It's a commitment to financial responsibility for a secure future. Proactive strategies are key to long-term success.

2 Tax Forgiveness Programs

Navigating the complexities of tax forgiveness can feel daunting, but understanding the process is the first step toward potential relief. Eligibility hinges on several factors, primarily demonstrating significant financial hardship that prevents you from meeting your tax obligations. This isn't simply claiming "I can't afford it," but rather providing concrete evidence—bank statements, pay stubs, medical bills, and documentation of unexpected job loss or major illness. The IRS, for example, looks for a consistent pattern of inability to pay, not just a single instance of financial difficulty. Thorough preparation is crucial for a successful application.

The application process itself involves completing IRS forms meticulously, providing all required documentation, and potentially undergoing an interview. Accuracy is paramount; errors can delay or even deny your application. Consider seeking assistance from a tax professional. They possess expertise in navigating the intricate regulations and can help assemble a compelling case. Remember to keep copies of everything submitted – this is vital for record-keeping and potential future references. Don't assume your application is automatically accepted after submission; proactive follow-up is key.

Many individuals, facing overwhelming tax debt, have successfully obtained forgiveness. These success stories aren't just anecdotal; they underscore the viability of the program for those who meet the strict criteria. For instance, a small business owner facing bankruptcy might qualify for forgiveness due to unforeseen economic downturns affecting their business. Similarly, individuals who experienced catastrophic medical expenses, or significant job losses leading to unemployment could also find success in seeking tax relief. These examples highlight the importance of documenting the circumstances fully and honestly. Remember, demonstrating genuine hardship is the cornerstone of a successful application. The program isn't a guaranteed path to forgiveness, but it presents a potential avenue for individuals facing insurmountable tax debts.

First, gather all relevant financial documents. This includes bank statements from the past several months, tax returns for the years in question, pay stubs, proof of income, and any documentation showing significant expenses such as medical bills or educational costs. Thoroughly review the instructions for the specific IRS form you're using. Prepare a detailed narrative explaining your financial situation, focusing on the reasons why you're unable to pay your taxes. Be honest and transparent; avoid embellishments or omissions that could jeopardize your application. The IRS scrutinizes applications closely, therefore, precision and honesty are critical.

Next, prepare a clear and concise summary of your situation. It should emphasize the reasons why you can't meet your tax obligations, without getting lost in excessive detail. Use plain language, avoiding jargon or complex financial terms. Ensure your explanation aligns perfectly with the supporting documentation you've provided. Consider seeking professional help; a tax professional can provide invaluable guidance in structuring your narrative and organizing the documentation. They can also advise on strategies to increase your chances of approval. This professional input can significantly enhance your application's persuasiveness and efficiency.

After submitting your application, track its progress. Be prepared for delays; the process can take time. Maintain regular contact with the IRS, inquiring about its status. If your application is denied, understand your options to appeal the decision. Gather additional evidence if necessary, and formulate a compelling argument to address the reasons for denial. Remember, the process can be complex, and persistence is often rewarded. Success hinges on thorough preparation, clear communication, and consistent follow-up. Persistence and attention to detail can make a significant difference in the outcome of your application.

2.1 Eligibility Criteria

Determining eligibility for tax forgiveness programs requires careful consideration of several key factors. The specific criteria can vary significantly depending on the program and the taxing authority involved. For example, a program designed to assist low-income individuals will naturally have different eligibility requirements than one aimed at businesses experiencing temporary financial distress. Understanding these nuances is crucial for a successful application. Remember that even if you believe you don't meet all criteria, a thorough review of the program's specifics and a consultation with a tax professional could reveal potential pathways towards qualification.

It's not enough to simply meet the minimum requirements; demonstrating a genuine need for relief is equally important. This often involves providing comprehensive financial documentation, such as bank statements, income tax returns, and proof of expenses. Think of it as building a persuasive case, not just filling out a form. Thorough documentation increases your chances of approval considerably, showcasing the depth of your financial hardship and the necessity of the tax forgiveness. In essence, you're presenting a narrative, not just a list of numbers. A poorly presented application, even with qualifying numbers, might be overlooked.

Different programs may emphasize different aspects of financial hardship. Some programs prioritize low income, focusing on a household's income relative to its expenses and basic needs. Others may focus on unforeseen circumstances, such as job loss, medical emergencies, or natural disasters, proving their impact on the applicant's ability to meet tax obligations. Still others may look at your ability to repay your debt, considering existing assets and potential future income. Understanding which criteria each specific program prioritizes is essential.

Before initiating an application, gather all relevant financial documentation diligently. This typically includes income tax returns for the past few years, bank statements, pay stubs, and supporting documentation for any claimed expenses or hardship circumstances. Maintain organized records; this meticulous organization prevents delays and strengthens your application. Consider creating a detailed timeline documenting the events leading to your inability to meet your tax obligations. This comprehensive documentation proves your financial situation's legitimacy to the reviewing authorities, enhancing your chances of approval.

The application process itself may vary, but many programs require an online or paper-based form, often involving a lengthy questionnaire. Be prepared to answer detailed questions about your income, assets, liabilities, and expenses. Accuracy is paramount; any false information could jeopardize your application and may result in penalties. It's advisable to allocate ample time to completing the forms meticulously and accurately. Remember, a complete and accurate application is your best asset.

Don't underestimate the value of seeking professional assistance. A tax advisor can assess your eligibility for various programs, guide you through the application process, and represent you during any appeals. While there is guidance readily available, navigating the complexities of the tax code requires expert knowledge that can mean the difference between success and failure. A tax professional can often identify eligibility for programs you might have otherwise overlooked. The cost of their services is often outweighed by the potential tax relief they can secure for you.

Finally, understand that the approval process can take time. Be patient and persistent; don't be discouraged if you don't receive an immediate response. Regularly check the status of your application and be prepared to provide additional documentation if requested. Communicate clearly and professionally with the relevant tax authorities throughout the process. Your persistence and proactive communication will demonstrate your commitment to resolving your tax situation, which may positively influence the decision-makers. Remember to keep records of all communication you have with the authorities, including dates, times, and the identities of the people you've spoken to.

2.2 Application Process

The application process for tax forgiveness programs can feel daunting, but breaking it down into manageable steps makes it less overwhelming. First, carefully review the specific requirements for the program you're applying to. Each program has its own eligibility criteria, and missing even one detail can delay or even deny your application. Gather all the necessary documentation well in advance. This might include tax returns, pay stubs, bank statements,

proof of income, and evidence of extraordinary circumstances that justify your request for forgiveness. The more organized and comprehensive your submission, the better your chances of success. Don't underestimate the importance of meticulous record-keeping; it's your strongest ally throughout this process.
Completing the application itself requires precision. Read every instruction thoroughly; pay close attention to deadlines, formatting requirements, and any specific questions that require detailed answers. Be honest and accurate in all your responses. False information can have serious repercussions, potentially disqualifying you from the program and even leading to further penalties. If you're unsure about anything, it's far better to seek clarification from the relevant tax authority than to make an assumption that could prove detrimental. Seeking assistance from a tax professional can be invaluable at this stage.
Once your application is complete, double-check every detail before submitting it. Ensure all supporting documents are included and correctly referenced within the application form itself. A well-organized application demonstrates your commitment and attention to detail, leaving a positive impression on the reviewing authority. Remember that a neatly presented application demonstrates professionalism and respect for the process, subtly enhancing your credibility. Missing documents, grammatical errors, or vague responses can hinder your application's progress. Proofread diligently. Consider having a friend or family member review your application for clarity and accuracy before sending it in.
After submitting your application, keep meticulous records of the date you submitted, the method of submission (mail, online portal, etc.), and any confirmation numbers you receive. This documentation proves you followed the prescribed procedure and will be valuable if there are any inquiries or delays. Be patient; the processing time for these applications can vary considerably, depending on the volume of applications and the complexity of your case. Regularly check the status of your application online or by contacting the relevant authority. Proactive monitoring demonstrates your commitment and helps ensure your application remains a priority. Don't hesitate to reach out if you don't receive updates within a reasonable timeframe. Active communication is crucial for ensuring a smooth process.
If your application is rejected, don't lose hope. Understand the reasons for the rejection and carefully consider whether you can address these issues. This

might involve gathering additional documentation, correcting any errors, or strengthening your case through a well-reasoned appeal. Appealing a rejection requires a thorough understanding of the reasons for the initial denial. Carefully analyze the rejection notice for specific points of contention. Addressing these points directly and providing substantiating evidence is crucial for a successful appeal. Remember, perseverance is key; sometimes a second attempt, armed with stronger evidence and a clearer presentation, leads to a favorable outcome. Consider consulting with a tax professional for guidance on the appeal process. They have experience in successfully navigating such situations and can provide valuable insights into strengthening your arguments and improving the presentation of your case. You are not alone in this; resources and assistance are available to support you in navigating this complex process.

Following these steps, while potentially challenging, significantly increases your chance of securing tax forgiveness. It's a process that requires patience, organization, and meticulous attention to detail. Remember that seeking professional guidance can be invaluable in ensuring you fulfill all requirements and present the strongest possible case. The rewards, however, often outweigh the effort involved, offering the chance for financial renewal and a brighter financial future. By methodically following these steps and remaining persistent, the possibility of tax forgiveness becomes more attainable and real. Remember that success in this matter often depends on the thoroughness and clarity of your submission. Your dedication to detail will greatly influence the outcome.

2.3 Success Stories

Many individuals, facing overwhelming tax debt, have successfully navigated the complexities of tax relief programs. Consider Sarah, a single mother of two who fell behind on her taxes due to unexpected medical bills. Initially paralyzed by fear, she discovered a local non-profit offering free tax assistance. With their guidance, she applied for a hardship waiver, meticulously documenting her medical expenses and reduced income. The IRS, acknowledging her circumstances, granted the waiver, significantly reducing her tax liability. Her story is a testament to the power of perseverance and seeking help. It underscores the importance of thorough documentation and clear communication with the tax authorities. Don't underestimate the impact of well-presented evidence.

Another inspiring case involves David, a small business owner who faced a crippling tax debt after a downturn in the economy. He initially felt defeated, believing that bankruptcy was his only option. However, a tax attorney advised him to explore an Offer in Compromise (OIC). This involved a careful assessment of his assets and liabilities, followed by a meticulously crafted negotiation proposal with the IRS. The proposal highlighted his current financial situation, demonstrating his inability to pay the full debt while outlining a realistic payment plan. Surprisingly, the IRS accepted his OIC, significantly reducing his tax burden and enabling him to restructure his business. David's successful negotiation underlines the importance of professional guidance in navigating complex tax situations and the potential for finding a mutually acceptable solution. Remember, meticulous preparation is essential for a strong negotiation.

Think about the experience of Maria, a self-employed consultant who fell behind on her quarterly tax payments due to inconsistent income. Initially, she felt overwhelmed and ignored several notices from the IRS. As penalties and interest accumulated, she sought the help of a tax professional. This professional quickly identified her eligibility for an installment agreement, helping her set up manageable monthly payments. While Maria still faced a significant debt, she managed to avoid more severe consequences such as wage garnishment or asset seizure. Her experience showcases that even small steps towards proactive problem-solving can produce significant positive results, delaying serious legal action. The key is early intervention and engaging the right professionals.

Sometimes success doesn't mean complete debt forgiveness. It can also involve preventing further penalties and creating manageable payment plans. Consider John, a contractor whose tax liability grew due to inaccurate bookkeeping. He proactively reached out to the IRS before serious consequences occurred and admitted his errors. The IRS responded favorably to his honesty and cooperated in establishing an installment agreement tailored to his limited income. This demonstrates that the proactive approach in resolving issues, even if it involves mistakes, can significantly reduce penalties and interest. Honesty and cooperation are vital.

The common thread connecting these narratives is proactive engagement, strategic planning, and resourcefulness. Each story exemplifies the power of understanding the system, seeking professional guidance when necessary, and remaining steadfast in the face of adversity. They highlight the value of thoroughly researching available tax relief programs. These real-life experiences encourage readers to approach their own tax problems with hope and a strategic mindset. Remember, even seemingly insurmountable challenges can be overcome with proper planning and expert assistance. These success stories emphasize that there is hope, even when tax debt seems insurmountable. Don't give up, explore all available options, and remember, professional help can be invaluable. While achieving success isn't guaranteed, the examples shared showcase that perseverance, accurate documentation, and proactive problem-solving will significantly increase the chances of successful tax debt resolution. Thoroughly review your options, seek professional guidance, and believe in the possibility of a successful resolution to your tax challenges.

3 Hardship Waivers & Appeals

Facing overwhelming tax debt can feel crippling, but remember, you're not alone. Many individuals find themselves in similar situations, and navigating the complexities of hardship waivers and appeals is achievable with the right approach. Understanding the process, however, requires careful planning and meticulous documentation.

Successful hardship waiver applications hinge on clearly demonstrating your inability to pay your tax liability without suffering significant financial hardship. This isn't merely stating you're struggling; it requires concrete evidence. Gather bank statements, pay stubs, medical bills, and any other documentation proving your limited income and substantial expenses. Be prepared to explain how the tax debt impacts your daily life, from jeopardizing your housing to limiting access to essential healthcare. The more comprehensive your presentation, the stronger your case.

Preparing a compelling appeal involves more than just restating your initial application. Think of it as a persuasive argument presented to a judge—because, essentially, that's what you're doing. Clearly articulate your financial situation, emphasizing the specific hardships you face. Don't shy away from details; use specific numbers and dates to support your claims. If you have already attempted to negotiate a payment plan and it proved unsustainable, document that as well. This shows your proactive attempts to resolve the debt before resorting to a more formal appeal. Remember, the goal is to present a clear and coherent narrative that convinces the tax authorities of your genuine hardship.

Often, overlooked is the importance of legal counsel. While you can certainly navigate this process independently, experienced tax professionals possess a deep understanding of tax law and procedures. They can help you identify all possible relief options, gather necessary documentation, and prepare a meticulously detailed appeal that addresses all the relevant legal points. A professional's expertise can significantly improve your chances of a favorable outcome, saving you time, stress, and potentially a substantial sum of money. This might seem like an added expense, but consider it an investment in protecting your financial well-being.

Don't underestimate the power of clear and concise communication. Your appeal shouldn't be a rambling collection of grievances; instead, structure it logically, presenting your arguments clearly and concisely. Use simple, direct language, avoiding jargon or overly technical terms. The goal is to communicate your hardship effectively and persuasively to someone who may not have a financial background. Think of the person reviewing your appeal as someone who needs the information laid out clearly, with supporting evidence readily available.

The timeline for processing hardship waivers and appeals can vary, depending on the complexity of your case and the agency involved. Therefore, it's crucial to be patient and persistent. Regularly follow up on your application's status to avoid unnecessary delays. Maintain detailed records of all communication with the tax authorities, including dates, times, and the names of the individuals you've interacted with. This will be invaluable should any questions or discrepancies arise later. Remember, persistence and organized documentation are key components of a successful appeal.

Beyond the immediate concerns of your current tax debt, consider this a learning experience. Analyze your past financial decisions, identifying areas for improvement in your budgeting, saving, and overall financial planning. Proactive financial planning, including consistently paying taxes on time, can prevent future tax issues and avoid the stress associated with hardship waivers and appeals. Establishing a system of financial accountability will benefit you well into the future. This includes setting a budget, tracking expenses, and saving a portion of your income regularly. These practices promote financial stability, reducing your vulnerability to tax-related problems in the future.

Remember, seeking help is not a sign of failure, but rather a sign of proactive financial management. Whether you choose to proceed independently or enlist professional assistance, keep in mind that your dedication to carefully documenting your circumstances and clearly conveying your financial hardships will significantly increase your chances of a successful outcome. The journey through hardship waivers and appeals can be demanding, but with diligence and the right approach, a resolution is certainly achievable. The information provided here aims to equip you with the tools to navigate this complex process effectively. The process can be daunting, but with the proper preparation and documentation, successfully navigating hardship waivers and appeals is certainly within reach.

3.1 Demonstrating Hardship

Convincing the IRS of genuine hardship isn't about melodrama; it's about presenting a clear, compelling picture of your financial struggles. Begin by meticulously documenting every aspect of your financial situation. This includes bank statements showing minimal balances, pay stubs reflecting low income, and medical bills or other significant expenses exceeding your ability to pay. Don't underestimate the power of detail; a simple statement of "I'm struggling" holds far less weight than a detailed accounting of your income, expenses, and assets. Remember, the goal is to paint a picture that leaves no doubt about the severity of your circumstances.

Your narrative must be honest and consistent. Discrepancies or exaggerations will instantly undermine your credibility. Presenting falsified documents, for example, can lead to severe penalties, far exceeding your initial tax debt. Therefore, focus on providing accurate and verifiable information. This honesty also extends to your explanations; be forthright about the reasons behind your financial difficulties, whether it's job loss, unexpected medical bills, or a natural disaster. Transparency, even when uncomfortable, builds trust and strengthens your case. Avoid vague statements or generalizations, backing every claim with solid evidence.

Beyond financial records, consider including supporting documentation that highlights the impact of your hardship. This could be letters from employers confirming job loss or reduced hours, eviction notices, or medical records detailing a prolonged illness. These documents provide tangible evidence of the challenges you face. Consider the emotional toll as well. While the focus is on financial hardship, you can briefly touch on the emotional stress caused by

your financial situation. This humanizes your situation and makes your case more relatable to the reviewing authorities. This isn't about emotional pleas, but about illustrating the holistic impact of the tax burden on your life.
Prepare a well-structured, concise letter explaining your situation. Avoid rambling or overly emotional language; instead, focus on presenting a clear, factual account of your circumstances and the reasons why you are unable to meet your tax obligations. Organize the letter chronologically, outlining the events that led to your current financial difficulty and clearly connecting those events to your inability to pay taxes. Maintain a professional and respectful tone, while conveying the urgency and seriousness of your situation. Proofread meticulously before submission; errors can undermine the credibility of your appeal. Remember, this letter is your primary tool for convincing the IRS of your hardship.
Seek professional help if needed. Navigating the complexities of tax laws and appeals can be challenging, and having an experienced tax professional on your side can significantly improve your chances of success. A professional can help you gather the necessary documentation, craft a compelling appeal, and present your case effectively to the IRS. They understand the nuances of the process, what constitutes sufficient evidence, and can anticipate and address potential objections from the IRS. Remember, this is a process; it might take time to build your case and demonstrate to the IRS the severity and genuineness of your hardship. Patience and persistence are vital. Don't give up hope if your first attempt isn't successful; sometimes, a second appeal with updated information can prove successful. The key is a meticulously crafted appeal based on your specific situation. Take advantage of all available resources and don't hesitate to seek professional guidance. Every case is unique, therefore, your preparation must be thorough and tailored to your specific circumstance. This will increase your likelihood of securing the tax relief you need.

3.2 Preparing Appeals

Gathering the necessary documentation is paramount. This isn't just about photocopying tax returns; it's about building a narrative. Think of your appeal as a story, a compelling account of your financial hardship. Include bank statements, pay stubs, medical bills—anything that paints a clear picture of your situation. Don't leave anything to assumption; provide concrete evidence to support every claim. Remember, the tax authorities need to see your struggle, not just hear about it. Specificity is crucial. Vague statements about "financial difficulties" won't cut it. Quantify your losses, detail your expenses, and explain how these factors have impacted your ability to meet your tax obligations. The more detailed your documentation, the stronger your case will be.

Your appeal letter itself must be clear, concise, and professional. Avoid emotional outbursts or accusatory language. Focus on presenting your case in a logical, objective manner. State your facts clearly, outlining the reasons why you are unable to meet your tax obligations. Reference specific legislation or IRS guidelines if relevant to strengthen your arguments. Many successful appeals effectively use specific legal precedents to bolster their claims.

Structure your letter logically. Start with a brief introduction, clearly stating your intent to appeal. Then, present your evidence systematically, linking each piece of documentation to a specific point in your argument. Conclude with a summary of your request and a clear statement of the relief you are seeking. A well-organized letter shows you are serious and prepared. Consider using bold headings to make key information stand out. A disorganized appeal might be overlooked.

Remember, you're not just pleading; you're presenting a case. Think critically about how your financial situation fits within the framework of IRS hardship guidelines. Research relevant IRS publications and case laws that might support your claim. Understanding these regulations is key to crafting a persuasive argument. This isn't simply about listing your problems; it's about demonstrating why you deserve relief under the existing regulations.

Legal counsel can be invaluable. While you can navigate the appeal process independently, an experienced tax attorney or enrolled agent can provide invaluable guidance. They can help you identify relevant case law, craft a compelling appeal letter, and represent you during any subsequent hearings. The cost of legal representation might seem daunting initially, but it could save you significantly more in the long run if your appeal is successful. Their expertise can mean the difference between success and failure.

Consider the timing of your appeal. Don't wait until the last minute. The process takes time, so it's crucial to begin preparations well in advance of any deadlines. Allow ample time for gathering documents, preparing your letter, and addressing any potential requests for additional information from the tax authorities. Promptness shows respect for the process and may favorably impact the outcome.

Throughout the process, maintain clear and consistent communication with the IRS. Respond promptly to all correspondence, and keep accurate records of all communications. This detailed record-keeping will become invaluable if your appeal requires further review or if there are any subsequent disputes. Even a minor detail, kept appropriately, can make a big difference. This careful attention to communication can help prevent misunderstandings or delays.

Finally, remember to remain persistent and positive. The appeals process can be lengthy and frustrating, but don't let setbacks discourage you. Stay focused on your goals and continue to advocate for your rights. The IRS acknowledges circumstances change. Keep pushing forward; your perseverance may lead to the positive tax resolution you are seeking. A positive and persistent approach can significantly influence the perception of your situation. Your dedication will show.

4 Installment Agreements

Negotiating an installment agreement with the IRS can feel daunting, but understanding the process can significantly ease the burden. First, you must determine your eligibility. Generally, you're eligible if you owe a combined total of income tax, penalties, and interest exceeding your ability to pay immediately. The IRS assesses your ability to pay based on your income, expenses, and assets. Thorough documentation is crucial; gather all relevant financial statements, bank records, and pay stubs to support your claim. Don't underestimate the importance of precise record-keeping at this stage.

Next, comes the application process itself. You can usually apply online using the IRS's online payment agreement system, a convenient and efficient method. The application will request detailed financial information, so be prepared to provide this promptly and accurately. Alternatively, you can submit a paper application. Whichever route you choose, ensure all the information is accurate and complete; inaccuracies can delay the process considerably, adding stress to an already stressful situation. Remember to keep copies of everything you submit.

Once the IRS receives your application, they will review it to determine your eligibility and the terms of your agreement. The terms will include the total amount owed, the monthly payment amount, and the repayment period. The monthly payment amount is calculated based on your demonstrated ability to pay; it shouldn't create undue financial hardship. The repayment period is generally flexible, typically ranging from 72 months, though extensions can sometimes be granted under specific circumstances. Understanding the IRS's criteria for determining payment amounts is crucial, so familiarize yourself with the relevant regulations and guidelines.

Failing to adhere to the agreed-upon payment schedule can have serious consequences. The IRS can impose penalties and interest on any missed payments. This can significantly increase your total debt and create a vicious cycle of mounting financial stress. Late payments may also lead to the revocation of the installment agreement and additional collection actions. Furthermore, the IRS may levy your bank accounts or place a lien on your property, causing significant disruption to your financial life. Therefore, consistent and timely payments are paramount. Budgeting carefully and automating payments when possible are excellent strategies to ensure consistent compliance.
The good news is, installment agreements are often modifiable. If your financial circumstances change significantly—for example, a job loss or unexpected medical expenses—you can request a modification of your agreement. You'll need to demonstrate these changes through supporting documentation, similar to the initial application process. The IRS will review your request, and based on your updated financial situation, may adjust your payment plan. However, don't expect immediate approvals; the process takes time and requires a diligent approach. Proactive communication with the IRS is key throughout this process, as this keeps them aware of any changing circumstances.
Finally, understand the implications of defaulting on your agreement. This usually leads to aggressive collection efforts by the IRS. This could include wage garnishment, bank levies, and even legal action. Defaulting, therefore, should be avoided at all costs. While the process of setting up and maintaining an installment agreement can seem intricate, the peace of mind that comes with a structured repayment plan is invaluable. Remember to keep meticulous records, communicate openly with the IRS, and seek professional advice when needed. Navigating these complex procedures effectively demands preparation and attention to detail; neglecting these aspects can result in serious consequences. Proactive planning can greatly mitigate risk, and by following these steps, you significantly enhance the likelihood of successful repayment. Remember, seeking help from a tax professional can prove invaluable in navigating this complicated process. They can offer invaluable guidance and support. They can assist in preparing all documentation accurately and also represent you if any issues arise with the IRS.

4.1 Setting Up Payments

Setting up an installment agreement with the IRS requires careful preparation and a clear understanding of your financial situation. Begin by gathering all necessary documentation, including tax returns, bank statements, pay stubs, and any other relevant financial records. This will demonstrate your current financial standing and support your application. It's crucial to be completely honest and accurate in your submissions; any discrepancies could jeopardize your chances of approval.

Next, you'll need to complete Form 9465, Installment Agreement Request. This form requests specific information about your income, expenses, and assets. Accurate completion is vital; providing false information could result in penalties. Don't rush; take your time to meticulously fill out each section to ensure accuracy. This process demands attention to detail to avoid delays or rejection. Take advantage of online resources and consider seeking professional help if you find the process overwhelming.

Once you've completed the form and gathered your documentation, you can submit your application either online through the IRS website or by mail. The IRS website provides helpful guides and frequently asked questions to assist you. Remember, the online process often provides faster processing times. However, mailing your application allows you to maintain a physical record. Weigh the pros and cons of each method before submitting.

The IRS will review your application, considering your financial situation and your ability to make regular payments. This review can take several weeks or even months, depending on their workload and the complexity of your case. During this period, it's essential to remain organized and maintain accurate records of all communication with the IRS. Patience is key, and proactive communication can help expedite the process.

Upon approval, you'll receive a formal agreement outlining the payment terms, including the monthly payment amount, the total number of payments, and the due dates. Meticulously review this agreement to ensure all details are correct. If you notice any inaccuracies or discrepancies, contact the IRS immediately to address them before you start making payments. This is important to avoid future complications and potential penalties.

Remember, maintaining consistent payments is crucial to avoid defaulting on the agreement. Missed payments can lead to significant penalties and potential legal action. Set up automatic payments or reminders to ensure you never miss a due date. Effective organization and proactive planning can alleviate unnecessary stress and prevent potential problems. Consider using budgeting tools to track income and expenses.

Moreover, throughout the duration of your installment agreement, your financial circumstances might change. If your financial situation significantly deteriorates, you should contact the IRS immediately to discuss modification options. They may be able to adjust your payment plan to reflect your changed circumstances, preventing a potential default. Proactive communication with the IRS is invaluable to avoid negative consequences.

Understanding your rights and responsibilities throughout this process is critical. The IRS provides ample resources and guidance on their website, and you should utilize these to your advantage. Should you encounter difficulties, consider consulting a qualified tax professional who can offer personalized guidance and support. This expertise can help you navigate the complexities of the process and avoid costly mistakes. Remember, seeking professional help is an investment in your long-term financial well-being. It provides crucial support and guidance that can help you achieve a successful outcome.

Finally, while an installment agreement offers a pathway to resolve your tax debt, remember it's a significant financial commitment requiring diligent adherence to the terms. Failure to meet your obligations could result in serious repercussions. Consistent communication, meticulous record-keeping, and careful planning are crucial for successfully managing your installment agreement and achieving financial stability. Remember that this is a process that requires constant attention and proactive effort to be truly successful. Maintaining open communication with the IRS is essential and should never be ignored.

4.2 Managing Installments

Careful planning is crucial for successfully navigating an installment agreement. Understanding the terms, including the total amount owed, the number of installments, and the due dates for each payment, forms the bedrock of effective management. Miss a payment, and you risk penalties. Therefore, meticulous record-keeping is paramount; maintain a detailed ledger noting each payment made, the date, and the method of payment. This detailed record will prove invaluable should any discrepancies arise. Furthermore, set up automatic payments to prevent accidental missed deadlines and alleviate the stress of manual tracking. Remember, proactive management minimizes the risk of default and its potentially serious consequences.

Regularly reviewing your agreement is a proactive step that safeguards against unforeseen difficulties. Life throws curveballs; unexpected job loss or medical emergencies can disrupt even the most carefully laid plans. Don't wait for problems to escalate. If you anticipate difficulties meeting your payment schedule, contact the relevant tax authority immediately. Open communication allows for exploring potential modifications to your agreement, preventing unnecessary penalties and preserving your financial stability. Proactive communication is key to mitigating potential risks, and it shows good faith. You'll likely find the authorities more willing to work with you if you reach out beforehand rather than after a missed payment.

Remember, an installment agreement isn't a get-out-of-jail-free card. While it provides breathing room, failing to adhere to its terms can lead to severe repercussions. Penalties for late or missed payments can quickly escalate, adding significantly to your total debt. These penalties vary depending on the taxing authority and the specifics of your agreement, so a clear understanding of the penalties associated with your particular agreement is vital before you sign anything. It's also wise to keep abreast of any potential changes in legislation that may impact your agreement.

Modifying an existing installment agreement might be necessary due to unforeseen circumstances. This process usually involves submitting a formal request to the relevant tax authority, clearly outlining your reason for needing an adjustment. The reasons may include a significant change in your financial circumstances, such as a job loss, unexpected medical expenses, or a major decrease in income. Supporting documentation, like proof of income or medical bills, will significantly strengthen your request. Be prepared for a thorough review of your application. Be patient, the process may take some time. Persistence and clear communication are key to a successful outcome.

Defaulting on an installment agreement should be viewed as a last resort. It carries significant consequences, including potential wage garnishment, bank levy, or even the seizure of assets. Before reaching this point, explore all possible alternatives. Open communication with the tax authority, as mentioned earlier, is crucial. They may be willing to work with you to find a mutually agreeable solution that avoids the severe repercussions of default. Consider seeking professional financial advice; a financial advisor can provide impartial guidance and help navigate complex financial challenges, exploring options beyond what you may have considered. The potential negative impacts of default are far-reaching and could severely damage your credit rating for many years.

4.3 Potential Penalties

Delinquency on an installment agreement carries significant consequences. The IRS isn't simply going to ignore missed payments; penalties accrue rapidly, impacting your already strained finances. These penalties can include interest charges, calculated daily on the unpaid balance, potentially escalating your debt substantially. Furthermore, you might face additional penalties for failure to file or pay, adding further layers of financial burden. Ignoring the issue will not make it disappear; it will only make it harder to resolve in the long run, deepening your financial hole. Understanding these repercussions is crucial for responsible management of your tax obligations.

Failure to adhere to your installment agreement's terms can result in the IRS revoking the agreement entirely. This drastic action means you'll be back to square one, facing the full, unpaid tax debt. The IRS then has the option to pursue further collection actions, including wage garnishment, bank levies, or even property seizure. These are serious consequences that could disrupt your life severely, even causing significant financial distress and legal complications. The severity of these actions is directly proportional to the level of your non-compliance. Therefore, diligent payment adherence is non-negotiable.

Beyond the direct financial penalties, the repercussions of defaulting on an installment agreement also have a profound impact on your credit score. A significant negative mark on your credit report makes it much harder to secure loans, mortgages, or even rent an apartment in the future. This can seriously limit your financial opportunities for years to come, hindering your ability to rebuild your financial stability. The long-term effects of a damaged credit

score can be far-reaching and deeply problematic for your overall financial health. Avoiding default is paramount for preserving your creditworthiness.
It's important to proactively address potential issues before they escalate into significant problems. If you anticipate facing difficulty in making a payment, contact the IRS immediately. Open communication is key; they may be willing to work with you to modify the agreement, potentially extending the repayment period or adjusting the payment amount to better suit your circumstances. Proactive engagement demonstrates your commitment to resolving the debt and significantly improves your chances of avoiding penalties and other negative consequences. Don't wait until you're already in default to seek help.
Remember, the IRS's primary goal isn't to punish taxpayers. They want to collect the taxes owed. By engaging with them early and openly discussing your financial challenges, you can often avoid the most severe penalties. Transparency and cooperation are vital. Working collaboratively to find a solution that works for both parties is always preferable to facing the repercussions of default. Building a relationship based on honest communication is far more effective than attempting to avoid the inevitable consequences of non-compliance. Remember, your proactive participation is key.
Even if your initial attempt to modify the agreement is unsuccessful, don't despair. Explore other options available. You may need to seek professional help from a tax advisor or attorney experienced in tax resolution. They can provide guidance on navigating the complexities of the IRS process and advocating for your rights. Their expertise can significantly increase your chances of success in reaching a favorable resolution. Do not underestimate the value of seeking professional assistance, particularly during challenging financial periods.
The potential penalties for non-compliance with an installment agreement are serious and far-reaching. From financial penalties and damaged credit to the potential seizure of assets, the consequences can be life-altering. Therefore, proactive planning, open communication with the IRS, and diligent adherence to the payment schedule are crucial for avoiding these negative outcomes. Remember, timely payment and honest engagement are your best defense against the significant risks associated with failing to meet your tax obligations. Your financial future depends on it. Seek help when needed. You're not alone in this.

4.4 Modifying Agreements

Circumstances change. Unexpected job loss, a medical emergency, or a sudden downturn in your business can significantly impact your ability to meet your installment agreement obligations. Fortunately, the IRS recognizes this reality and offers pathways to modify existing agreements. Don't panic; explore your options proactively. Reaching out early shows good faith and increases your chances of a positive outcome.

Initiating the modification process is relatively straightforward. You'll typically need to complete Form 9465, Installment Agreement Request, providing detailed documentation of your changed circumstances. This isn't merely a formality; presenting a convincing case requires thorough preparation. Compile all relevant financial documents, such as updated bank statements, pay stubs, and medical bills, to support your claim. These documents paint a vivid picture of your current financial reality, helping the IRS assess your situation accurately. Remember clarity and precision are crucial; avoid ambiguity.

The IRS will review your request, examining the supporting documents carefully. This process can take time, so be patient and persistent. Frequent follow-up is generally discouraged, unless you have significant new information to report. Regular communication however, might be beneficial, depending on your particular circumstances and the IRS representative's responsiveness. Always keep records of all communications, both written and verbal. This meticulous record-keeping can be invaluable should any misunderstandings or disputes arise later.

Once the IRS has reviewed your request, they will inform you of their decision. They may grant a modification, adjusting the payment amount, extending the payment period, or offering alternative solutions. Alternatively, they may reject your request, potentially outlining reasons for the denial. If your request is rejected, don't give up. Understand the reasons for the rejection, and assess the possibility of resubmitting a revised request with stronger supporting documentation or a more compelling narrative. Remember, persistence can often pay off. A second attempt may incorporate additional documentation demonstrating even more severe financial hardship.

Modifying an installment agreement isn't merely about altering payment terms; it's about navigating a crucial financial crossroads. Understanding the process and your rights is paramount. The IRS's website offers extensive resources, but a tax professional's guidance can prove invaluable. A qualified professional can help you navigate the complexities of the application process, ensuring your application is thorough, accurate, and persuasive. They can also represent you throughout the process, improving your chances of a successful outcome, and lessening the emotional burden of dealing with the IRS directly. Navigating this process requires a proactive and organized approach. Maintain open communication with the IRS. Respond promptly to any requests for additional information, and remember to keep detailed records of all interactions. Proactive communication prevents misunderstandings and delays. Your detailed documentation, demonstrating a genuine need for modification, significantly increases your chances of a favorable outcome. Do not underestimate the power of clear and concise communication. Express your situation in a respectful and professional manner, demonstrating your commitment to fulfilling your tax obligations to the best of your ability.

Remember that seeking professional help does not denote weakness; it shows a commitment to resolving your financial challenges effectively. Tax laws are intricate, and having an expert guide you can prevent costly mistakes and ensure you're utilizing all available avenues for relief. The peace of mind offered by professional guidance is worth the investment, allowing you to focus on addressing your financial difficulties without the added stress of navigating complex regulations and procedures independently. This proactive approach, coupled with a clear understanding of the process, can often make the difference between success and failure.

Consider exploring all available options. While modifying an existing agreement is often the preferred path, exploring other options simultaneously might prove beneficial. Perhaps a hardship waiver is also applicable, offering additional relief. Simultaneously pursuing multiple avenues might yield better results. Remember to remain patient, persistent, and well-organized throughout the entire process.

The consequences of failing to modify your agreement can be severe. Defaulting on your installment agreement can lead to significant penalties, including further interest charges, wage garnishment, and even levies on your bank accounts or assets. These consequences can have a devastating impact on your financial well-being. Preventing such a scenario requires proactive planning

and consistent communication with the IRS.
Therefore, understanding the process of modifying installment agreements is essential. It's a vital part of managing your tax obligations effectively, particularly during periods of financial hardship. By utilizing the available resources and seeking professional assistance when necessary, you can navigate this process successfully and avoid the potentially damaging consequences of defaulting on your agreement. Remember, proactive engagement and meticulous preparation are key elements in a successful modification. Your future financial well-being depends on it. Take the necessary steps, and secure your financial stability.

4.5 Defaulting on Agreements

Defaulting on an installment agreement carries serious consequences. It's not a decision to take lightly, and understanding the ramifications is crucial before even considering it. The IRS isn't forgiving; missing payments triggers immediate action, potentially leading to wage garnishment, bank levy, or even property seizure. These actions can significantly disrupt your financial life, creating far more problems than the original tax debt. The repercussions are immediate and severe. You're not just dealing with late fees; you risk damaging your credit score, making it significantly harder to obtain loans or credit cards in the future. This impacts not only your immediate financial situation but also your long-term financial health. The negative effects can linger for years, impacting your ability to secure mortgages, rent apartments, or even get a job in some sectors.
Your actions have direct repercussions. Remember, the IRS will pursue all available legal avenues to recover the outstanding debt. They aren't going to simply write off the debt; instead, they are highly skilled at locating and accessing your assets. This may involve contacting your employer, freezing your bank accounts, or placing liens on your property. They have extensive powers at their disposal, and they're not afraid to use them. Ignoring the situation will only exacerbate the problem; the debt will grow with penalties and interest, making it progressively harder to resolve. Procrastination in this area is detrimental. Active engagement, even if it seems overwhelming, is far better than avoidance.

Before defaulting, consider all alternatives. Exploring options like modifying your existing agreement is essential. Perhaps you've experienced a sudden change in circumstances – job loss, illness, or unexpected expenses – making your current payment schedule unmanageable. The IRS often works with taxpayers who demonstrate genuine hardship. Contacting them and explaining your situation is your first step. They might be willing to adjust your payment plan, reducing the monthly amount or extending the repayment period, making it more feasible for you to meet your obligations. Documentation substantiating your hardship claim is crucial to support your appeal for a modification. Don't simply assume a modification isn't possible; proactively pursuing one could prevent a default and the devastating consequences that follow.

Re-evaluating your budget is another crucial step before considering default. Prioritize essential expenses, identify areas where you can cut back, and explore additional income streams. This might involve seeking part-time employment, selling unnecessary assets, or reducing discretionary spending. Every little bit helps. Even small adjustments can make a significant difference in your ability to manage payments. A professional financial advisor can offer expert guidance in creating a sustainable budget and identifying additional income sources, particularly in challenging financial situations. Thoroughly assessing your financial picture gives you a more accurate understanding of your options.

If default is unavoidable, seek professional help immediately. A tax attorney or enrolled agent can guide you through the process, helping you understand your rights and the options still available, even after a default. They can negotiate with the IRS on your behalf, potentially mitigating the penalties and preventing the most severe consequences. While the consequences of default are serious, seeking professional help can minimize the damage. Remember, you're not alone; many people face similar situations. This isn't a shameful secret; it's a financial challenge that requires professional expertise. Navigating this complex landscape requires careful planning and informed decision-making. Professional guidance can alleviate some of the stress and uncertainty.

The IRS offers various programs designed to assist taxpayers experiencing financial difficulties. Exploring these programs is essential before resorting to default. They are not always easy to navigate, and obtaining the necessary assistance might necessitate professional guidance; you can get the most out of your efforts by having someone qualified helping you. It is not a passive process; it requires engaging actively with the IRS, presenting your case effectively, and providing complete and accurate documentation. Remember, thorough preparation is key to a successful outcome. Failing to do so can leave you facing further penalties and a more difficult path to resolution. Default should be viewed as a last resort, after exhausting all possible alternatives. Proactive steps now can safeguard your financial future.

5 Offer in Compromise (OIC)

An Offer in Compromise (OIC) is a legally binding agreement between you and the IRS. It allows you to settle your tax debt for a lower amount than what you originally owe. This isn't a magical solution; it's a serious financial maneuver requiring careful consideration and preparation. Think of it as a last resort, a lifeline when other options have proven insufficient. Successfully navigating this process hinges on understanding its complexities and strategically presenting your case.

Your eligibility for an OIC depends on several factors. The IRS assesses your ability to pay your tax liability fully, considering your current income, assets, and expenses. They'll scrutinize every detail, so be prepared to be completely transparent. Don't try to hide assets or underreport your income; this could severely damage your chances and even lead to further penalties. Honest and complete disclosure is paramount. They analyze your current financial situation, comparing it to the total tax debt. The goal is to show them that paying the full amount is truly beyond your means, and that an OIC represents the best feasible outcome for both parties. They look for a demonstrable inability to pay. This isn't merely about difficulty; it's about proving genuine financial hardship.

Negotiating an OIC requires a strong understanding of your financial position and the IRS's expectations. Gather comprehensive documentation, meticulously detailing your income, expenses, and assets. Bank statements, pay stubs, tax returns – nothing should be left out. Remember, the IRS is looking for consistency; discrepancies will undermine your credibility. A well-prepared and organized submission significantly increases your chances of a favorable outcome. Preparing the documentation yourself isn't recommended;

seek a qualified tax professional. They understand the intricacies of the process and can represent your case effectively. They can also help you assess the viability of an OIC and develop a negotiation strategy.

The negotiation itself is a delicate dance. It's not about demanding a lower amount; it's about presenting a compelling narrative that resonates with the IRS. Clearly and concisely demonstrate your financial hardship, highlighting the inability to pay the full balance. Highlight extraordinary circumstances if applicable. Your aim is to convince the IRS that an OIC is the most realistic and equitable solution for both parties. Be prepared to provide further details and explanations, and anticipate their questions. Transparency and openness are key.

The IRS will evaluate your offer based on several factors including your ability to pay, the amount of the liability, and the collectibility of the debt. They assess your current income, assets, and living expenses to determine your realistic payment capacity. Factors like your age, health, and dependents can be considered if they significantly impact your ability to repay. The IRS will also examine the age of the tax debt, as older debts are often considered more difficult to collect. There's no guarantee of acceptance; they might reject your offer, asking for a revised proposal or simply declaring the original debt uncompromisable. If they reject your first attempt, don't despair, this is fairly common, and often a revised offer, strengthened by further evidence and negotiation, will be favorably received.

Once the IRS receives your OIC proposal, they'll thoroughly review it. The process can take several months. During this waiting period, patience is vital. You should continue to maintain meticulous financial records and be prepared to provide additional information if requested. A positive response will relieve a significant burden; a rejection will necessitate reevaluation of your financial strategy and perhaps a consideration of alternative approaches. Careful planning and a strategic approach are key to a successful OIC. The acceptance or rejection of your offer dictates the next steps. Acceptance means a legally binding agreement to pay a reduced amount, concluding the tax debt issue. Rejection may require revisiting other options explored in previous chapters, including installment agreements or further appeals. Remember, professional assistance dramatically increases the likelihood of a favorable outcome, allowing you to focus on rebuilding your financial stability.

5.1 OIC Eligibility

Determining eligibility for an Offer in Compromise (OIC) requires careful consideration of several key factors. The IRS assesses your ability to pay your tax liability based on your current income, expenses, and assets. They don't simply look at your current financial snapshot; they analyze your future financial prospects as well, projecting your ability to make payments over a reasonable period. This forward-looking approach is crucial, as the IRS aims to reach a fair and sustainable resolution. Therefore, gathering comprehensive financial documentation is paramount; this includes bank statements, pay stubs, tax returns, and any other evidence demonstrating your financial situation. Don't overlook details; accuracy is vital.

Understanding your equity in assets is crucial. The IRS considers assets like real estate, vehicles, and investments. They'll want to know the current market value of these assets, deducting any outstanding debts against them to determine your net equity. If you have significant equity, it could impact your OIC eligibility, as it demonstrates a potential capacity for repayment. However, remember to present a realistic, complete picture of your financial state, avoiding any attempts to conceal or minimize assets.

Your income plays a significant role in OIC eligibility. The IRS examines your income from all sources—employment, self-employment, investments, and other income streams. They look at your income history, projecting future income to assess your capacity for repayment. It's crucial to honestly present your current and projected income, showcasing the stability or instability of your income. Don't underestimate the value of meticulously documenting income fluctuations, temporary employment gaps, or any other relevant factors affecting your income. This transparency demonstrates your commitment to honest dealings.

Expenses are just as important as income. The IRS will analyze your necessary living expenses, such as housing, food, transportation, medical bills, and child support payments. They'll want to see detailed breakdowns of these expenses, verified through documentation like receipts, bank statements, and lease agreements. Supporting this financial data with specific explanations adds further credibility. Carefully documenting and justifying these expenses is crucial, as it showcases that your living costs are genuinely necessary and reasonable for your situation. Remember to avoid unnecessary or extravagant expenses; presenting a realistic, lean budget strengthens your application.

Beyond the quantitative aspects of income and expenses, the IRS also assesses your overall financial situation. This qualitative assessment considers factors such as job security, recent job losses, unexpected health issues, or other extenuating circumstances. They want to understand the context of your financial difficulties, acknowledging that life events can significantly impact an individual's ability to meet their tax obligations. The more thoroughly you articulate these circumstances, the more effectively you'll demonstrate your inability to meet your tax burden.

Preparing a comprehensive OIC application requires meticulous attention to detail. Accurately portraying your financial situation through thorough documentation is vital. Remember, omissions or inaccuracies could negatively impact your chances of acceptance. Consulting with a qualified tax professional can prove invaluable, providing guidance in preparing a strong and convincing application. Their expertise in navigating the complexities of OIC eligibility can significantly increase your chances of a favorable outcome. Their support in preparing a complete and accurate application greatly improves your chances. Proactive and honest preparation enhances your credibility and makes your OIC application stronger. Remember, the process requires considerable preparation and documentation.

Finally, navigating the OIC process often involves considerable patience and persistence. The IRS reviews applications carefully, and the process can take several months. Maintaining open communication with the IRS throughout the process and addressing any requests for additional information promptly are vital for a successful outcome. Regular follow-ups can accelerate the process while demonstrating your active engagement. Remember, the goal is to arrive at a mutually acceptable solution, which often benefits from proactive communication and a willingness to collaborate. The final step is awaiting the decision, maintaining open communication until the process reaches a conclusion.

5.2 Negotiating an OIC

An Offer in Compromise (OIC) represents a significant opportunity to resolve substantial tax debt, potentially reducing your liability to an amount you can realistically afford. Successfully negotiating an OIC requires a meticulous approach, combining a thorough understanding of your financial situation with strategic communication with the IRS. Remember, preparation is key.

Before initiating negotiations, meticulously gather all your financial documentation. This includes bank statements, pay stubs, tax returns, and any other records that demonstrate your current income, assets, and expenses. Presenting a comprehensive picture of your financial reality is crucial to establishing credibility and supporting your proposed settlement. Don't underestimate the importance of accuracy and completeness; any omissions can significantly weaken your position. Remember to organize these documents logically for easy review.

The initial communication with the IRS should be professional and well-articulated. A well-crafted letter, clearly outlining your circumstances and proposing a reasonable OIC amount, is an effective first step. Avoid emotional language or unsubstantiated claims. Instead, focus on presenting factual data that objectively supports your inability to pay the full tax liability. Emphasize your commitment to resolving the debt responsibly. The letter should set the tone for a cooperative, yet firm negotiation.

Your proposed OIC amount should be based on a realistic assessment of your ability to pay. Consider factors such as your disposable income, available assets, and reasonable living expenses. Utilize readily available IRS resources and perhaps consult a tax professional to determine a feasible offer. Low-ball offers might be rejected outright, while excessively high offers fail to demonstrate your genuine hardship. Finding the optimal balance is critical to a successful negotiation.

Navigating the negotiation process may involve several iterations of communication with the IRS. Be prepared to provide additional documentation, answer questions thoroughly, and potentially adjust your proposed offer based on their feedback. Maintain clear, consistent communication. Avoid delaying their requests for information, and respond promptly and professionally to each communication. Remember, responsiveness reflects your seriousness in resolving the matter.

The IRS may counter your initial offer with a different amount. Evaluate their counteroffer carefully; assess its feasibility against your financial capacity, and be prepared to negotiate further. A successful OIC negotiation often involves compromise from both sides. Maintain a professional and respectful demeanor throughout the process. Remember, patience and persistence are vital elements for a successful outcome.

The acceptance or rejection of your OIC will be communicated formally in writing. If your offer is accepted, it's legally binding, and it is critical to make all payments according to the agreed schedule. If your offer is rejected, understand the reasons provided and consider your next steps, which might include appealing the decision or exploring alternative payment arrangements. Don't be discouraged by a rejection; it doesn't necessarily signal the end of your options.

Throughout the entire OIC negotiation, maintain accurate records of all communication, submitted documentation, and payment transactions. This organized documentation will be valuable not only during the negotiation process but also as proof of your good faith effort and compliance should any disputes arise later. Proactive record-keeping safeguards you against potential issues.

Remember, negotiating an OIC is a complex process. While this chapter provides practical guidance, consulting with a qualified tax professional is strongly recommended. They possess the expertise to navigate the intricacies of the IRS regulations and to help you develop a well-supported strategy tailored to your unique circumstances. Remember, seeking professional assistance can significantly improve your chances of success.

5.3 Acceptance & Rejection

The IRS's decision on your Offer in Compromise (OIC) can feel like a life-altering event. Acceptance brings immense relief, a fresh start, and the chance to rebuild your financial future. Rejection, however, can be devastating, leaving you feeling defeated and facing the daunting prospect of continuing to grapple with a significant tax debt. Understanding both possibilities, the reasons behind them, and the subsequent steps is crucial. It's not merely about the immediate outcome; it's about navigating the emotional and practical consequences and strategizing for future action.

A successful OIC hinges on effectively demonstrating your inability to pay your full tax liability. The IRS meticulously examines your financial situation, looking at your income, expenses, assets, and liabilities. They assess your ability to repay the debt through traditional methods like installment agreements. If they determine that the proposed OIC settlement is fair and in line with their guidelines, reflecting your true ability to pay, they will likely accept your offer. This acceptance will drastically reduce your tax burden, freeing up significant resources for other financial priorities, such as paying off other debts and building a stable financial future. This process, while arduous, offers a pathway towards stability.

Conversely, an OIC rejection can stem from several factors. Perhaps your financial documentation wasn't sufficiently persuasive, or the proposed payment wasn't considered low enough given your demonstrated financial standing. Maybe you missed crucial deadlines or failed to provide necessary supporting evidence. Sometimes, the IRS may require additional information or clarification before making a final decision. This is not necessarily indicative of failure, but rather an indication that more thorough and precise documentation is needed to solidify the case. Rejection isn't the end of the road, but it does require immediate action.

Upon receiving a rejection, carefully review the IRS's explanation, identifying areas where your application fell short. Was your income understated? Did you overestimate your expenses? Were there critical documents missing? Consult with a tax professional immediately; they can help you understand the reasons for the rejection and determine whether a strong case can be made for reconsideration. They can also help you to prepare a well-structured appeal which demonstrates a comprehensive understanding of the IRS's assessment and offers amended supporting documentation. A thorough analysis of what went wrong and how to remedy it is critical to a successful re-submission.

Don't let the emotional weight of rejection overwhelm your strategic thinking. Remember, the IRS's decision isn't necessarily final. You have options. You can appeal the decision, providing additional evidence and addressing any deficiencies highlighted in the rejection notice. You might need to revise your financial data. Even a small adjustment in your submitted information could make a significant difference in the final outcome. Persistence and strategic preparation are your key weapons.

Consider exploring alternative payment options, such as an installment agreement, if the OIC route proves unsuccessful. While not offering the same level of debt reduction as an OIC, an installment agreement provides a structured repayment plan that can alleviate the immediate pressure of a large tax debt. This option provides a much-needed break in the cycle of accumulating interest. It's crucial to understand the terms and potential penalties associated with an installment agreement to avoid defaulting.

Regardless of the IRS's decision, professional guidance is essential. A skilled tax professional can interpret the complexities of tax laws, navigate bureaucratic processes, and advocate on your behalf. They can act as a buffer, explaining difficult legal language in plain terms and ensuring you're fully equipped to understand your options. Remember, they have experience in handling these scenarios, and their expertise is invaluable to make informed decisions. Seeking professional help isn't a sign of weakness; it's a strategic move to protect your financial future. Their experience will provide reassurance during what can be an emotionally challenging time.

Remember, the process of seeking tax relief is often long and complex. It demands patience, perseverance, and a willingness to meticulously gather and present your financial information. Acceptance or rejection of your OIC is just one step, albeit a critical one, in a journey toward resolving your tax debt. Focus on learning from each step, ensuring you're prepared for potential challenges and ready to adapt your strategy when needed. The ultimate aim is to develop a stable financial plan that not only resolves this immediate tax burden but prevents similar issues from arising in the future.

6 Alternative Payment Options

Facing a substantial tax debt can feel overwhelming, but remember, you're not alone. Many resources exist to help you manage and potentially reduce your tax burden. This chapter explores options beyond the installment agreements and Offers in Compromise we've already discussed, focusing on alternative payment strategies tailored to individual circumstances. Careful consideration of your unique financial situation is key to selecting the most appropriate approach.

Short-term solutions can provide immediate relief, offering breathing room to strategize long-term solutions. These often involve negotiating with the IRS for an extended payment plan or exploring options like a short-term loan to cover immediate tax liabilities. Remember, communication is paramount; actively engaging with the IRS and clearly outlining your financial difficulties can significantly influence their willingness to accommodate your needs. Obtaining a short-term loan should only be a last resort, and you must carefully weigh the interest rates and repayment terms to avoid adding to your existing financial strain. Thorough research into reputable lenders is essential.

For long-term solutions, consider consolidating debt. This involves combining multiple debts, including your tax liability, into a single monthly payment. While this simplifies your financial management, it's vital to carefully compare interest rates and terms across different consolidation options to avoid getting trapped in a high-interest cycle. Consider seeking professional financial advice before pursuing this route; a financial advisor can help you determine if debt consolidation aligns with your long-term financial goals. Failing to thoroughly review the details of any debt consolidation plan could lead to unforeseen consequences that negatively impact your financial future.

Understanding your legal rights and responsibilities concerning tax debt is crucial. The IRS is bound by certain regulations and procedures, understanding these procedures can empower you in your interactions with them. Never sign anything you don't fully understand; seek clarification from a tax professional before committing to any agreement. Remember, navigating the complexities of tax law can be challenging, and seeking professional assistance shouldn't be seen as a sign of weakness but rather a strategic move to ensure you're making informed decisions that protect your financial well-being.

Engaging a tax professional or financial advisor is a proactive step that can significantly improve your odds of a positive outcome. These professionals possess in-depth knowledge of tax laws, regulations, and available relief programs. They can analyze your specific financial situation, identify potential avenues for tax relief, and assist in navigating the complexities of the application process. A professional can also help you negotiate effectively with the IRS, ensuring your rights are protected and advocating for a fair resolution. The initial investment in professional help can save you substantial amounts of money and stress in the long run. Their expertise can help prevent costly mistakes, ensuring you make the best decisions for your financial health.

Remember, navigating tax debt requires patience, persistence, and a strategic approach. While the process can be stressful, remember that help is available. By taking proactive steps, such as seeking professional assistance and fully understanding your options, you can work towards resolving your tax liability and securing your financial future. The initial investment in professional assistance can significantly mitigate future financial risks, ultimately safeguarding your financial well-being. The journey to resolving tax debt might be challenging, but through informed action and professional guidance, you can achieve a positive resolution. Don't hesitate to explore every avenue available, and remember, your financial future is worth fighting for. Thoroughly researching and understanding the implications of each decision you make is vital for long-term financial stability. Every step you take toward a solution strengthens your position and brings you closer to financial freedom. Taking a proactive approach not only alleviates current financial pressure but also sets a foundation for sound future financial management. Consider this journey a learning experience, building financial literacy for a more secure future. Learning from this experience helps you avoid similar difficulties in the future and strengthens your financial foundation. The knowledge gained throughout this process will be invaluable in future financial planning and decisions.

6.1 Short-Term Options

When facing an immediate tax burden, short-term solutions can provide crucial breathing room. These options aren't necessarily long-term fixes, but they can prevent immediate penalties and offer time to develop a more comprehensive strategy. Consider them a bridge to a more stable financial future, not the destination itself. Remember to always prioritize open communication with the relevant tax authority.

One such option involves negotiating a short-term payment plan. This isn't the same as a formal installment agreement, which typically involves a structured, longer-term payment schedule. Instead, a short-term payment plan might involve agreeing to pay a portion of your tax liability immediately, with the remainder due within a significantly shorter timeframe than a formal installment agreement. The feasibility of this approach depends heavily on your individual circumstances and the tax authority's willingness to cooperate. Successfully negotiating a short-term plan often hinges on demonstrating your current financial constraints and outlining a clear plan to resolve the outstanding debt within the agreed-upon timeframe. Clear documentation of your income, expenses, and assets is crucial for this process. Don't forget to meticulously record every communication with the taxing authority.

Another viable short-term strategy might include temporarily liquidating assets. This could involve selling some investments, possessions, or other assets to raise the immediate funds needed to satisfy a portion of the tax debt. However, proceed cautiously, as this approach may have long-term ramifications depending on your asset portfolio. Carefully assess the potential short-term gains against any potential long-term losses before making any decisions. Consider the tax implications of selling assets, as capital gains taxes could add further complexity. It's often beneficial to consult with a financial advisor to determine the most tax-efficient methods for liquidating assets. Remember to weigh the short-term benefits against any potential long-term financial implications.

For those experiencing genuine hardship, exploring hardship waivers remains a strong possibility. While not strictly a short-term payment plan, obtaining a hardship waiver can provide crucial relief by temporarily suspending or reducing your tax obligations while you navigate difficult financial circumstances. Successfully demonstrating hardship usually involves providing compelling evidence of unexpected and significant financial setbacks – job loss, medical emergencies, or natural disasters, for example. This process can be intricate and requires thorough documentation. Don't overlook the importance of assembling a comprehensive case that clearly communicates your financial distress and its direct impact on your ability to meet your tax obligations.

It's important to acknowledge that short-term options are not always a panacea. They can provide temporary reprieve, allowing you time to secure long-term solutions. However, they are not a substitute for addressing the underlying financial issues causing the tax debt. Failing to address the root causes may only lead to recurring problems in the future. Therefore, while implementing short-term solutions, proactively work toward developing a long-term financial plan to prevent similar situations from arising again.

Furthermore, remember that each case is unique. The effectiveness of short-term strategies depends entirely on your specific financial circumstances, the nature of your tax liability, and the flexibility of the relevant tax authority. Open and honest communication with the tax authority is paramount throughout this process. Providing accurate and complete information strengthens your position and increases the likelihood of a successful outcome. Don't hesitate to seek professional assistance from a tax advisor or financial planner. They can provide tailored guidance, ensuring you make informed decisions based on your unique situation. They can help you navigate complex regulations and potentially negotiate better terms with the authorities. Their expertise can be invaluable in finding the optimal solution for your individual circumstances. The added cost of professional help can be significantly offset by the benefits of achieving a favorable resolution.

Ultimately, strategically deploying short-term solutions offers a crucial opportunity to gain some breathing room and work toward a more sustainable long-term financial strategy. Understanding your options, carefully evaluating their implications, and seeking professional guidance when necessary, will maximize your chances of successfully navigating your tax burden and achieving long-term financial stability. Proactive planning, consistent communication, and a well-defined strategy are essential for effectively addressing and resolving your tax challenges. Remember, acting promptly and decisively can often make a significant difference in the outcome.

6.2 Long-Term Strategies

Developing a robust long-term strategy for managing your tax liabilities requires a proactive and multifaceted approach. It's not simply about resolving immediate issues; it's about building a system that prevents future tax problems and safeguards your financial well-being for years to come. This involves meticulous record-keeping, a clear understanding of your tax obligations, and consistent engagement with your financial situation. Ignoring these aspects can lead to accumulating debt and increasing stress, making it significantly more difficult to navigate future challenges. A preventative mindset is far more effective than reactive firefighting.

Careful tax planning is crucial. This isn't about finding loopholes but rather about understanding the tax implications of your financial decisions. Consult with a qualified tax professional to create a personalized strategy that accounts for your specific circumstances, income level, and anticipated financial changes. Regular reviews, perhaps annually or even semi-annually, are vital to ensure your plan aligns with your evolving situation and takes advantage of any relevant legislative changes or updates. Proactive planning allows for flexibility, adjustments and prevents unexpected tax burdens.

Maintaining detailed and organized financial records is paramount for long-term success. This includes keeping accurate records of all income, expenses, and relevant tax documents. Digital solutions can significantly streamline this process, helping you stay organized and readily access the necessary documentation when needed. Remember, having readily available information will reduce stress during tax season or when facing an audit, and allows for more efficient and effective planning. A well-organized system prevents delays and simplifies future interactions with tax authorities.

Establishing a budget and sticking to it is essential for managing your finances effectively. A clear budget allows you to track your income and expenses, identify areas where you might be overspending, and allocate funds for tax payments. This discipline helps prevent unexpected financial shortfalls that can lead to tax debt. Budgeting software or simple spreadsheets can aid in this process. The key is to create a realistic budget that reflects your spending habits and income patterns while leaving room for unexpected expenses, thus mitigating the risk of financial emergencies that often exacerbate tax problems.

Regularly reviewing your tax situation allows for early detection of potential problems. This proactive approach allows you to address issues before they escalate into significant financial burdens. Even small discrepancies or overlooked deductions can accumulate over time, creating larger problems later. Regularly reviewing your tax situation prevents unforeseen issues. Think of it as a routine health check for your finances – preventative care is much less expensive than emergency treatment.

Explore tax-advantaged savings and investment options. These strategies can significantly reduce your tax burden over the long term. Such options range from retirement accounts to education savings plans, each with its own set of rules and benefits. Understanding and utilizing these accounts can allow for significant tax savings that compound over time. A tax professional can guide you in selecting the best options for your financial situation and long-term goals. Proper utilization of these options significantly reduces your tax liability over time.

Seek professional assistance when needed. Navigating the complexities of the tax system can be challenging, and professional help is invaluable for developing and implementing effective long-term strategies. Tax professionals can provide personalized advice, manage your tax filings, and advocate on your behalf if you encounter problems with tax authorities. The cost of professional assistance is often outweighed by the potential benefits of avoiding costly mistakes or unnecessary financial burdens. Don't hesitate to seek professional advice – it's a worthwhile investment in your financial future.

By integrating these long-term strategies into your financial planning, you can significantly improve your ability to manage your tax liabilities, reduce stress, and secure a more stable financial future. Remember, consistency and proactive planning are key to achieving lasting financial well-being. This holistic approach encompasses not just the immediate resolution of tax issues, but also the development of sound financial habits and strategies that will benefit you for years to come. It's an investment in your peace of mind and financial security. The effort you put in now will yield significant rewards in the future.

6.3 Seeking Professional Help

Navigating the complexities of tax relief can be daunting, even with a thorough understanding of the available programs and strategies. That's why seeking professional help is often the most crucial step towards a successful resolution. A qualified tax professional, such as an enrolled agent, CPA, or tax attorney, possesses the specialized knowledge and experience necessary to analyze your unique financial circumstances and guide you toward the optimal solution. They understand the intricacies of tax law, the nuances of various relief programs, and the negotiation tactics required when dealing with taxing authorities. This expertise can be invaluable in saving you time, stress, and potentially significant amounts of money.

Their skills extend beyond simple paperwork. They can meticulously organize your financial documents, ensuring everything is presented accurately and completely. This attention to detail can significantly improve your chances of a favorable outcome. A professional will also help you effectively communicate with the IRS or other relevant tax agencies. They understand the language of tax law and can articulate your situation persuasively, potentially leading to a more favorable settlement. Think of them as your advocate, navigating the bureaucratic landscape on your behalf and ensuring your voice is heard effectively.

Beyond the technical aspects, a professional's support provides invaluable peace of mind. Dealing with significant tax debt is stressful; the emotional toll can be considerable. Having a skilled professional manage the process allows you to focus on other crucial aspects of your life, reducing stress and maintaining stability. Their expertise ensures that you're not making critical mistakes that could worsen your financial situation. Remember, a seemingly small oversight can have significant consequences, and a professional can help you avoid such pitfalls. They are skilled in identifying potentially overlooked options or strategies that you might miss on your own. This could be anything from a specific tax credit to an alternative payment arrangement tailored to your circumstances.

The cost of professional help is a significant consideration, but remember, it's an investment, not an expense. The potential savings from avoiding penalties, interest, or even a lengthy legal battle can far outweigh the fees charged for professional assistance. Moreover, many professionals offer initial consultations at reduced rates or even for free, allowing you to assess their expertise and decide if their services are right for you before committing to a larger fee. Thoroughly research the professional's qualifications, experience, and client testimonials before making a commitment. This is crucial for ensuring a good fit and maximizing your chances of a favorable outcome. Look for professionals specializing in tax resolution or those with proven success in handling cases similar to yours.

Remember, choosing the right professional is crucial. Don't hesitate to interview several candidates before making a decision. Ask about their experience, their success rate, and their approach to resolving tax issues. A good professional will listen carefully to your situation, answer your questions thoroughly, and provide a clear roadmap for resolving your tax debt. Avoid professionals who make unrealistic promises or guarantee specific outcomes; responsible professionals will be upfront about the challenges and potential outcomes. Choosing a professional is often about finding the right fit—someone who is not only skilled but also approachable, understanding, and responsive to your concerns. This personal connection can be a vital factor in navigating the complex and often stressful process of tax debt relief.

Selecting a professional is a significant decision, one that can significantly impact the outcome of your tax relief efforts. Remember, their expertise extends beyond just filing paperwork; they offer valuable guidance, support, and advocacy throughout the entire process. They act as a buffer between you and the often intimidating bureaucracy of the tax system, offering peace of mind and the knowledge that your case is being handled by someone with extensive expertise. Taking this step can prove to be one of the most effective measures you can take towards securing your financial future and eliminating the burden of tax debt. They possess the skill to effectively navigate the intricacies of tax law, negotiate favorable settlements, and ultimately, help you regain control of your finances. Don't underestimate the power of professional assistance in your journey towards tax relief. It's a vital investment in your financial well-being, offering the best chance for successful resolution.

7 Conclusion: Securing Your Financial Future

Maintaining consistent tax compliance isn't merely about avoiding penalties; it's about building a solid foundation for long-term financial security. Think of it as constructing a house: a weak foundation leads to cracks and instability, while a strong one ensures resilience against the inevitable storms. Proactive tax planning is the bedrock of this financial house, ensuring stability and growth. This means understanding your tax obligations, accurately recording your income and expenses, and filing your returns on time, every time. Regularly reviewing your financial statements and seeking professional advice when needed allows for early detection of potential issues, preventing small problems from escalating into significant tax debts. Consider it preventative maintenance for your financial well-being; just like regular check-ups for your health, proactive tax management is crucial for your financial health. The peace of mind that comes from knowing you're on solid financial ground is invaluable.

Budgeting is more than just tracking income and expenses; it's a strategic tool for aligning your spending with your financial goals. Effective budgeting allows you to prioritize essential expenses, save for the future, and gradually eliminate unnecessary spending. By creating a realistic budget that reflects your lifestyle and financial situation, you gain control over your finances and reduce the likelihood of future tax burdens. Consider using budgeting apps or spreadsheets to track your income and expenses; these tools can simplify the process and provide insightful visuals of your spending habits, revealing areas where you can cut back or reallocate funds. Regularly reviewing and adjusting your budget ensures it aligns with your changing financial circumstances, maintaining fiscal responsibility. Ultimately, disciplined budgeting prevents impulsive spending, promoting financial stability and reducing the risk of accumulating debt, which directly impacts your tax situation.

Effective financial planning goes beyond immediate tax concerns; it's about building a future where financial stability isn't just a goal, but a reality. This involves creating a comprehensive financial plan that incorporates both short-term and long-term objectives. Short-term goals might include paying down debt or creating an emergency fund, while long-term goals could include saving for retirement or purchasing a home. Understanding the interplay between your financial goals and your tax obligations is crucial for making informed decisions that benefit both your immediate and future financial well-being. Regularly reviewing and adjusting your financial plan, particularly when significant life events occur, will ensure it aligns with your current circumstances and aspirations. With careful planning and consistent effort, you'll not only secure your financial future but also alleviate potential tax-related stress.

Seeking professional advice is not a sign of weakness, but a testament to smart financial management. A qualified financial advisor can provide personalized guidance based on your specific circumstances, helping you navigate the complexities of tax planning and financial management. Their expertise can prove invaluable in identifying opportunities for tax savings and implementing strategies for long-term financial growth. Consider the cost of professional advice as an investment in your financial future, a crucial step toward building long-term stability and security. They can also offer a fresh perspective, spotting potential issues you may have overlooked and suggesting solutions you might not have considered. Don't hesitate to reach out for professional assistance; it's a proactive measure that can significantly benefit your financial health and reduce future tax-related challenges. It's a form of insurance against financial instability, offering guidance and support to navigate the complexities of financial planning and tax management.

Remember, the journey to securing your financial future is a continuous process, requiring consistent effort and proactive planning. By applying the strategies outlined in this book, including diligent tax compliance, effective budgeting, and thoughtful financial planning, you will significantly reduce your tax burdens and create a stronger foundation for lasting financial security.

Embrace financial responsibility as an ongoing commitment, not a temporary fix. Regularly review and adapt your strategies, seeking professional guidance when needed. The reward for your dedication will be a future characterized by financial stability, freedom, and the peace of mind that comes from knowing you've taken control of your financial destiny. Ultimately, proactive financial management isn't just about managing your taxes; it's about shaping a brighter and more secure financial future for yourself and your loved ones. The path to financial success is paved with consistent effort and informed decisions.

7.1 Maintaining Tax Compliance

Maintaining consistent tax compliance isn't merely about avoiding penalties; it's about fostering a healthy financial relationship with the relevant tax authorities. Proactive tax management minimizes future complications, contributing to long-term financial stability. This involves diligent record-keeping, accurate reporting, and timely filing of all necessary tax returns. Understanding your individual tax obligations is paramount, and seeking professional advice when needed is a sign of fiscal responsibility, not weakness. Don't be afraid to ask for clarification on complex regulations; clarity avoids costly mistakes. Regularly review your tax situation, perhaps annually or even quarterly, depending on your business complexity. This allows you to identify and address potential issues before they escalate into significant problems. Use tax software or hire a tax professional to help navigate the complexities, ensuring accuracy and compliance. Modern tax software often provides reminders about upcoming deadlines and flags potential problems based on your entered data. A qualified accountant can offer more personalized guidance and strategy, tailored to your specific circumstances.

Accurate record-keeping is fundamental to successful tax compliance. Maintain detailed records of all income, expenses, deductions, and credits. Organize these records systematically, utilizing digital tools or physical filing systems, whichever suits your preferences. Consistency is key – employ the same method each year to streamline the process. Well-organized records simplify the preparation of your tax returns and facilitate easier audits, if necessary. Remember, the goal isn't just to meet the legal minimum; it's to create a clear and auditable picture of your financial activities.

Understanding the specific tax laws applicable to your circumstances is crucial. Tax laws vary based on location, income type, and numerous other factors. Consulting relevant publications or seeking professional advice ensures you're operating within the legal framework. Ignoring tax laws can lead to severe consequences, including substantial penalties and interest. Staying informed about current legislation ensures your practices remain compliant. Moreover, proactive awareness allows you to leverage tax advantages legally available to you, maximizing your financial well-being.

Develop a budget and stick to it. A well-structured budget allows for better financial forecasting, aiding in accurate tax estimations. Understanding your income and expenses helps in planning for tax payments and prevents unexpected tax burdens from disrupting your financial flow. Regularly monitoring your budget enables timely adjustments, ensuring you always have sufficient funds allocated for tax obligations. Effective budgeting contributes significantly to financial stability and reduces the risk of tax-related stress. A well-planned budget allows for proactive savings and investments, further strengthening your long-term financial security.

Plan for your tax liabilities throughout the year, not just during tax season. This involves setting aside a portion of your income regularly for anticipated tax payments. Regular savings prevent sudden, large tax payments from creating financial hardship. This proactive approach reduces stress and ensures a smoother financial year. It's like establishing a 'tax savings account' throughout the year, ensuring preparedness when tax deadlines approach. Consider the use of tax-advantaged accounts and investment vehicles as a long-term strategy for wealth building and tax minimization.

When facing challenges or uncertainties, don't hesitate to seek professional tax advice. Tax laws are complex, and navigating them alone can be daunting. A qualified tax advisor offers valuable expertise, personalized guidance, and potentially significant cost savings in the long run. They can assist in tax planning, preparing returns, and addressing tax-related issues. Their insights can prevent costly mistakes and ensure your strategies align with current tax regulations. Remember, proactive tax planning is a sign of responsible financial management, not an added expense. Professional assistance can actually save you significantly in the long run by optimizing your tax situation.

Finally, remember that maintaining tax compliance is an ongoing process, not a one-time event. Regular reviews, accurate record-keeping, and proactive planning are essential for long-term financial health. Treat tax compliance as an integral part of your financial management strategy, not merely as a yearly obligation. By adopting a proactive approach and seeking assistance when needed, you can foster a positive relationship with the tax authorities, ensuring financial stability and peace of mind for years to come. The effort invested in proactive tax management significantly outweighs the potential consequences of negligence.

7.2 Planning for the Future

Proactive tax planning is crucial; it's not just about reacting to problems but preventing them. Imagine a ship navigating treacherous waters – a skilled captain anticipates storms and charts a safe course, not just reacting to the waves that crash. Similarly, proactive tax planning involves forecasting potential tax liabilities and developing strategies to mitigate them. This involves understanding your income sources, deductions, and credits, and regularly reviewing your tax situation. Regular meetings with a tax professional can help you stay ahead of potential issues. This ensures you're taking advantage of all available tax breaks and minimizing your tax burden over time. Don't underestimate the power of careful financial management.

Consider diversifying your income streams. This could involve exploring multiple employment opportunities, investing in passive income ventures, or even starting a side business. Diversification safeguards against the risks associated with a single income source, providing greater financial stability and a buffer against unexpected expenses. When your financial situation is secure, you're better equipped to manage unexpected tax obligations, whether those are related to your employment or otherwise.

Building an emergency fund is not just a wise financial move; it's a powerful tool for tax relief preparedness. Unexpected events can greatly influence one's financial capabilities, and the emergence of unexpected tax obligations can quickly spiral into severe financial distress. Having a financial safety net in place, usually about three to six months' worth of living expenses, can provide crucial breathing room should unexpected tax liabilities arise. This buffer protects against the need for drastic measures to address tax debts, such as taking out high-interest loans or neglecting essential expenses.

Retirement planning is another facet of future financial security. Tax-advantaged retirement accounts like 401(k)s and IRAs offer significant benefits, not only by promoting saving for retirement but also through tax deductions or deferrals. These benefits lessen your current tax burden while simultaneously building long-term wealth. It's a proactive strategy that addresses both immediate and long-term financial wellbeing, securing you a comfortable retirement with less financial strain. Regular contributions to your retirement account become a form of automatic tax saving.

Regularly review and update your financial plans. Your circumstances may change over time: income levels fluctuate, family status alters, and your long-term goals evolve. Annual reviews, or even more frequent ones depending on significant life changes, allow you to adapt your strategies. This ensures your financial and tax plan remains aligned with your ever-changing goals and reduces the likelihood of facing significant tax liabilities unexpectedly. This proactiveness empowers you to make timely adjustments, maximizing your tax relief opportunities.

Finally, don't hesitate to seek professional guidance. A qualified financial advisor or tax professional can provide personalized advice tailored to your unique circumstances. They can help you navigate complex tax laws, identify opportunities for tax savings, and develop a comprehensive financial plan that encompasses all facets of your financial health, including your tax liabilities. This expertise can prevent costly mistakes and ensure that you're taking full advantage of all available options for managing your tax obligations. Remember, proactive planning is an investment in a more secure and stable financial future.